A Pug's Guide to
Good
Manners

A Pug's Guide to
Good
Manners

LESSONS IN LIFE FOR THE
WELL-ROUNDED PUG

Gemma Correll

DOG 'n' BONE

This edition published in 2023 by Dog 'n' Bone Books
An imprint of Ryland Peters & Small Ltd

20–21 Jockey's Fields   341 E 116th St
London WC1R 4BW   New York, NY 10029

www.rylandpeters.com

10 9 8 7 6 5 4 3 2 1

First published in 2013 as *A Pug's Guide to Etiquette*

Text © Gemma Correll 2013
Design and illustration © Dog 'n' Bone Books 2013

A CIP catalog record for this book is available from the
Library of Congress and the British Library.

ISBN: 978-1-912983-74-2

Printed in China

Designer: Jerry Goldie
Illustration: Gemma Correll

Art director: Sally Powell
Creative director: Leslie Harrington
Head of production: Patricia Harrington
Publishing manager: Penny Craig
Publisher: Cindy Richards

CONTENTS

INTRODUCTION

An ancient breed descended from the Chinese *Lo-Chiang-Sze* dog, the pug is a proud, handsome, and fragrant creature. He is the loveable champion of the canine world. A snorting, wheezing, farting ambassador for small dogs; not much bigger than a cat, yet exhibiting the sturdy rotundness of an unusually excitable warthog. Bred many centuries ago by the monks of Tibet, beloved pet of royals and aristocrats including Queen Victoria and Marie Antoinette, and muse to artists such as William Hogarth, the modern pug must strive to honor his legacy as a special, superior creature.

Custom emphatically dictates that a well-bred pug should abide by the strict rules of etiquette and decorum. Navigating this potential minefield of manners may initially prove difficult for a young pug not yet experienced in the conventions of polite society, but he will quickly discover the satisfaction that following the rules can bring. He must realize that actions such as begging for food, molting all over the sofa, and relieving himself on the grumpy neighbor's front lawn are essential facets of pug protocol. It is simply not proper to behave like a common dog—the pug is a different breed altogether. He should understand the matters of socializing, courting, and licking, and, above all, seek to conduct himself in a winsome and unwaveringly squishy fashion.

A pleasant manner comes naturally to the pug, born as he is to the possession of good looks, a pleasant temperament, and an excellent knowledge of where the food is to be found. The pug's duty is to amuse and entertain his human;

to greet him or her with enthusiasm on their return from an outing, however fleeting (even a short bathroom visit is worthy of at least ten minutes of frantic jumping and yelping); and to make himself useful in a variety of ways. He must strive to maintain a facade of utter melancholy, masking an inner world positively brimming with love, joy, and undigested kibble. The well-bred pug understands that he must undulate between manic tomfoolery and near-catatonic sleepiness, endeavoring to maintain a steady 20 hours of sleep per day. He will do well to heed the pug's motto, *Carpe Kibble* (or "Seize the Kibble") and remember that foremost covenant of Pugdom:

You may lead a pug to water, but you cannot make him have a bath.

The Famous Pug Head Tilt

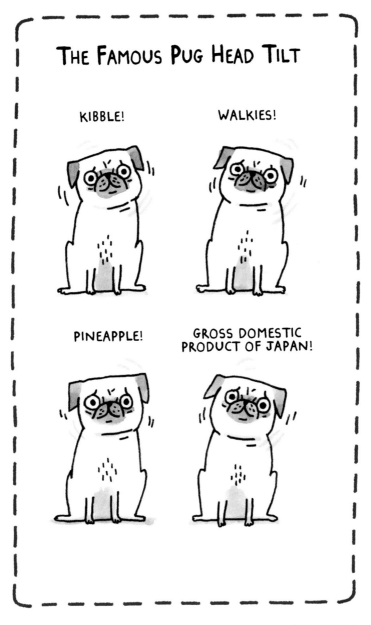

KIBBLE!

WALKIES!

PINEAPPLE!

GROSS DOMESTIC PRODUCT OF JAPAN!

CHAPTER 1

PERSONAL APPEARANCE & GROOMING

THE GOLDEN RULE

Lick. Lick often; lick thoroughly. Lick until you can lick no more. Lick the air if necessary.

ANATOMY OF THE GENTEEL PUG

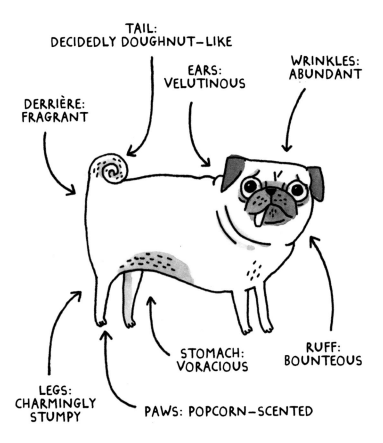

TAIL:
DECIDEDLY DOUGHNUT-LIKE

EARS:
VELUTINOUS

WRINKLES:
ABUNDANT

DERRIÈRE:
FRAGRANT

LEGS:
CHARMINGLY
STUMPY

PAWS: POPCORN-SCENTED

STOMACH:
VORACIOUS

RUFF:
BOUNTEOUS

REGARDING PUG HAIR

A well–bred pug is altruistic and magnanimous
with his favors, bestowing generous gifts of
hair unto his home and unto his human.

GROOMING

Grooming is of the utmost importance and can be quite pleasurable.

Nail Clipping

A nail clipping session should never be submitted to without a vehement and obstreperous display of one's vexation.

COMPLETING ONE'S TOILETTE

It is conduct unbecoming of a pug to complete his ablutions in private.

On Sunbathing

A pale belly is positively vulgar. Any opportunity to sunbathe should be immediately seized upon.

ATTIRE: DRESSING IN STUPID OUTFITS

It is an unfortunate fact of life that many humans are wont to dress innocent pugs in ridiculous outfits. When submitting to these indignities, it is important to maintain a stiff upper lip and air of nonchalance at all times.

SELECTING A NOM DE PLUME

Cultivate a mysterious and alluring personality by adopting many pseudonyms.

BATH TIME

A genteel pug is never guilty of the sin of
allowing his human to bathe unchaperoned.

Regarding the Cone

A well-bred pug maintains his dignity, even at times of utmost discomfiture.

THE ART OF CONVERSATION

It is of great importance, in the formation of good manners, that a young pug should be accustomed to mingle in polite society.

CHAPTER 2
PUGS AT HOME

THE MORNING ROUTINE: WAKING UP

THE PAW IN THE FACE

Upon rising, preferably at a suitably early hour, you should ensure that you tread most thoroughly upon the face, bosom, and genitals of your sleeping owner.

THE EAR LICK

THE PARP

THE SUFFOCATION

THE MORNING ROUTINE: CLOSED DOORS

In the home, a blocked entryway or thoroughfare must never be tolerated. Should one be encountered, it is advisable to scratch at the obstruction and whine pathetically. Once the door is opened for you, however, do not feel obliged to use it.

THE MORNING ROUTINE: LEAVING THE HOUSE

MEALTIMES: TAKING CHARGE

It is imperative that you preside over all activity that takes place in the kitchen. The ideal position for satisfactory supervision is directly beneath the cook's feet.

MEALTIMES: THE KIBBLE

To maintain a healthy digestive system, from time to time eat at speed so that you may then immediately puke the contents of your stomach upon the expensive Persian carpet.

Mealtimes: Timetable

A strict mealtime regime and timetable must be adhered to. Breakfast and dinner should be served no later than one minute after the specified time. In the event of a delay, you are permitted to theatrically voice your grievances.

USEFUL SERVICES

A well-bred pug endeavors to make himself indispensable to his human by providing a variety of useful services.

BOOK REST

SPA TREATMENTS

LICK

MASSAGE

PILLOW WARMING

OW
OWW
OWWW

ENTERTAINING

SNORING

It is a pug's prerogative to snore, to snore loudly, and to snore continuously.

IN THE BEDROOM

A well-bred pug will always play the buffoon, even when sleeping. He should twitch extravagantly and make unusual noises, preferably while drooling profusely.

PUG POSITIONS

THE GRUMP

THE LOAF

THE BELLY RUB?

THE YAWN 'N' STRETCH

THE SLUMP

THE SPRAWL

THE SYMPATHY VOTE

THE CHIN REST

THE PAW TUCK

THE DOWNWARD
FACING PUG

THE FROG

THE TWIST'N' SNIFF

THE SLUMP O'GUILT

THE HEAD TILT

THE SIT-UP

THE KITTY

THE PENSIVE
PAW LICK

THE NEW FRONTIER

THE THINKER

THE CROSSOVER STRETCH

THE SIDE
SLUMP

THE HANG-OUT

CHAPTER 3

ENTERTAINING

APERITIFS

Tissues, procured from your guests' pockets and handbags, make delightful appetizers.

TABLE MANNERS

A respectable pug will ensure that for the duration of a meal he is seated immediately below the human guest considered most likely to drop tidbits.

CLEANING

It is looked upon as the height of vulgarity to allow any leftover food to remain on the crockery.

WATERING HOLE

The usual social graces are considered
unnecessary at the watering hole, where
it is advisable to push your way in and
make as much mess as possible.

Entertaining Guests

During any respectable dinner party, your guests will appreciate a well-formed poo, or noisy bum-licking display, in the middle of the dining room.

ON FARTING

It is considered polite to fart heavily after your host has served you a meal.

BATHROOM BREAKS

Follow all guests to the bathroom. Do not wait for an invitation—they will welcome your presence.

After Dinner Entertainment

Upon finishing dinner, you may wish to instigate a rousing game of "Repeatedly Pushing One's Ball Under the Chair" or "Stealing Things from the Laundry Basket."

TOY DISPLAY

When entertaining guests, a pug of good breeding will always demonstrate a display of his toys.

Parlor Tricks

"SIT"

"PAW"

"HIGH FIVE"

"UP"

"SPIN"

"SPEAK"

Humans, in their infinite feeble—mindedness, will be impressed by even the smallest repertoire of tricks. Do not give up your skills too freely—encourage them to bribe you with treats and belly rubs.

CHAPTER 4

SPORTS & RECREATION

THE PILE UP

On your introduction to society, it is highly recommended that you acquaint yourself with your fellow pugs by taking part in a traditional "Pile Up."

TOY TEST

SNIFF TEST

CHIN REST INSPECTION

TASTE TEST

QUALITY CONTROL

ENDURANCE TEST

APPROVED!

When offered a new toy, do not immediately pounce upon it—this is considered the very height of bad manners. Instead, perform a series of rigorous tests in order to ascertain the toy's worthiness of being added to your repertoire.

PLAYTIME

A well-bred pug will find amusement in the following activities...

suckle

TOY SUCKLING

scoot
scoot

BUM SCOOTING

wriggle
wriggle

CATCHING AND EATING
LIVE SPIDERS

THE CUSHION BULLDOZING GAME

FLUFF

Chasing tiny bits of fluff is a healthful and pleasant means of diversion.

FETCH

Never play "Fetch"—this evinces lack of
proper manners and is better left to
creatures of a lower social standing,
such as Labradors and humans.

OVEREXERTION

Strenuous exercise should be kept to a minimum, with the obvious exception of the thrice daily doctrinal "Pug Run."

Making Calls

When paying a social call, a pug should make himself entirely familiar with every corner of the host's abode.

Bidding Farewell

SHE IS GOING TO **LOVE** THAT HALF—CHEWED PIG'S EAR I LEFT ON HER PILLOW.

Having paid his adieux, a polite pug will always endeavor to leave a small parting gift for the host, who will doubtless be delighted to chance upon it (preferably whilst barefoot) some minutes later.

CHAPTER 5

ETIQUETTE OF THE STREET

BARKING

It is considered highly appropriate to bark whenever you feel that it is necessary and at absolutely any time of the day or, indeed, the night.

On occasion, a pug should bark for no discernable reason at all.

YOU MAY BARK AT:

TRASH BAGS

INANIMATE OBJECTS

BIG, SCARY—LOOKING DOGS

SMALL CHILDREN

THE VACUUM CLEANER

YOUR SHADOW

In Regard to Inclement Weather

A pug of good breeding does not trouble himself to leave the house when it is raining.

PUDDLE AVOIDANCE

Nor does he acquiesce to traverse a puddle.

THE DAILY CONSTITUTIONAL

The search for the perfect spot for your morning evacuation should be at your leisure and should always exceed ten minutes in length. Especially if it is snowing.

Poop Dance

Upon the completion of your aforementioned duties, it is customary to perform a dance.

Fig 1: Kick (x3)

Fig 2: Kick (x3)

Fig 3: Freestyle

Street Salutations

You should recognize acquaintances with a courteous bum sniff and face lick.

Strangers may be greeted with either frenzied, cacophonous barking or gratuitous snogging. Use your discretion.

Encountering the Ignoramuses

A pug may find himself accosted by poorly educated peasants who make impolite insinuations regarding his breeding and apparent similarity to "That dog off *Men in Black*." Take pity on these poor inerudite souls, for they do not know any better.

Drop & Roll

Fig. 1

Fig. 2

Fig. 3

Upon encountering something which appears
to be dead or rotting, the recommended
action is the "Stop, Drop, and Roll" routine,
as detailed above.

SNIFFING

One of the foremost pleasures in a young pug's life is the delicious sniffing of morning air, which should be inhaled deeply and appreciated like a fine bowl of puddle water.

A Final Word

Above all, remember that, as a pug, you were born a fundamentally superior creature and are therefore the true master of any respectable household.

And don't let them forget it.

ACKNOWLEDGMENTS

All my love and gratitude to Anthony—my husband, studio partner, and coffee-drinking buddy—and to my ever-supportive family. And of course to Mr Pickles and Bella; my tiny, stinky little muses, whose etiquette is never less than perfect.

Thanks to everyone at Dog & Bone and Cico Books, especially Pete Jorgensen, and to my pals at The Little Red Roaster, Norwich, for supplying me with delicious caffeinated drinks and baked goods.